Getting Started with your Halogen Oven

The Halogen Oven is an excellent tool to have in your kitchen
cooking a diverse range of foods which means the possibilitie
aims to guide you along your way, giving you recipes and har
will give you confidence and pleasure in using your Halogen (
this is a rough guide and ensure that all food is cooked thorou

High Rack - used for grilling - **Low Rack** - used for roasting

Extender Ring - used to give an even heat and slow down the cooking process.
Particularly good for foods you don't want to grill but need to cook with an even heat.

Cookware - We use a variety of dishes, tin and glass oven dishes (that can also be
used under a grill) when cooking in the Halogen Oven. (You can use silicon bake ware,
however I do advise that you only use in temperatures up to 180 degrees and only on
the lower rack with the extender ring to avoid burning).

Grilling on the High Rack - Rough guide

Chops - 6-8 minutes each side - Chicken breasts - 8-10 minutes each side
Bacon - 3-5 minutes each side - Burgers - 8-10 minutes each side
Steaks – Rare 2-5 minutes each side - Medium 5-7 minutes each side - Well done 7-10
minutes on each side. (Remember the amount of time also depends on the thickness
of your steak).

Cooking Vegetables - Root Vegetables

Place on a tray with oil on the low rack - Temp 240 degrees - Time 30 minutes (turning
every 7 or until cooked). Other Vegetables - wrap in tin foil, adding a little water to the
foil to help steam them (such as broccoli) on whichever rack you are cooking on for 15
minutes or until cooked.

Cooking Meat

When cooking meat joints it's best to opt for larger, thinner pieces of meat as these cook
faster than compact meat joints (which tend to take longer to cook through to the centre).

Chicken Small 2-3lb/ Medium 3-4½lb - Cook on low rack and turn every 10-15 minutes
to ensure even and thorough cooking. Cook at 220 degrees for 45 minutes* then 180
degrees for a further 45 minutes, for a medium sized chicken cook for a further 10
minutes or until juices run clear after piercing with a knife.

Lamb Joint - 3lb/1½kg - Cook on a low rack - Cook at 240 degrees for 10 minutes, turn
and cook for further 10 minutes* then cook at 180 degrees for 60 minutes, turn every 15
minutes and cook for further 30 minutes if required well done.

Pork joint - 2lb/1kg (rub with salt prior to cooking) - Cook on a low rack at 220 degrees
for 60 minutes, turn every 15 minutes* then cook at 180 degrees for further 30 minutes.
Check juices run clear by piercing with a knife - continue cooking till juices run clear.

Beef Joint - 2lb/1kg - Cook on low rack at 240 degrees for 30 minutes, turn every 10
minutes* then cook at 180 degrees for 10 minutes = rare/blue, 30 minutes = medium or
50 minutes = well done.

*** you can add your par boiled potatoes and vegetables to the Halogen Oven for
roasting at this point.**

Halogen Cooking Made Simple
Paul Brodel & Dee Hunwicks
CONTENTS

Starters / Appetizers:

Main Courses / Entrée:

Main Courses / Entrée: (Continued)

PAGE

Desserts:

Handy Hint
Instead of mustard use pesto in the cream cheese.

Asparagus and Parma Ham Wraps

Ingredients
16 asparagus spears
4 tbsp cream cheese
2 tbsp mayonnaise
½ tbsp favourite mustard
4 sheets parma ham
½ tbsp fresh parsley (chopped)
2 tbsp gruyère cheese (grated)
Pinch salt
Pinch pepper
Serves 4

Method
1. Put the asparagus in a suitably sized bowl and pour over boiling water. Leave for five minutes.
2. Mix the cream cheese, mayonnaise, mustard and fresh parsley together and season with salt and pepper.
3. Place parma ham in the oven dish and put four asparagus spears in each ham slice, top each with the cream cheese mixture. Wrap the ham over the filling sprinkle with grated gruyère cheese.
4. Grill on high wire rack at 240°C/460°F for 6 minutes or until golden brown.
(When using a regular oven place on high grill setting for 6 minutes until cooked).

7

Handy Hint
You can use your preferred cheese instead of stilton.

Avocado Fans with Bacon and Stilton

Ingredients

2 ripe avocadoes
50g / 2oz stilton
3 streaky bacon rashers (chopped)
Rocket leaves to garnish
Serves 2 / 4
**Serve with crusty bread and
rocket / arugula salad.**

Method

1. Cook chopped bacon under the halogen grill for 5 minutes until
crispy on full power 240°C / 500°F .
2. Peel and fan avocados and place on oven dish.
3. Put the stilton and bacon on top of avocado and cook on high rack at
240°C / 500°F for 5 minutes until cheese is bubbling.
4. Serve with crusty bread and rocket / arugula salad.
(When using a regular grill make sure you pre-heat the grill and follow
method above.)

9

Handy Hint
Add fried garlic or chopped olives at stage 5
for a different flavoured bread.

Basic Bread Rolls

Ingredients

250g / 9oz plain or bread flour
½ tsp salt
1 tsp sugar
40g / 1½oz melted butter or oil
¼ pt / 160ml warm milk
15g / ½ oz fresh dried yeast
 (if using dried yeast use ½ the amount)
Flavourings:
Garlic / Olives / Sun-dried Tomato
Serves 4

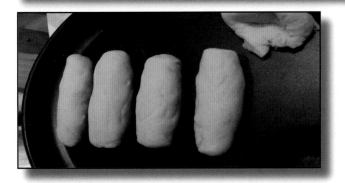

Method

1. Mix the yeast with the milk and sugar, leave for six minutes.
2. Place the flour and salt into a bowl and mix in the melted
butter. Add the yeast liquid and mix to a soft dough.
3. Knead the dough for ten minutes until it becomes firm and elastified,
(stretchy). To save time you can use a food mixer with a dough hook.
4. Place the dough into a bowl and cover with a clean damp cloth. Leave
in a warm place for ten minutes, the dough will expand.
5. Knead the dough again for two minutes, to reduce it to the original
size, you can add any flavourings to your bread now.
6. Decide what shape bread you are going to make and place in an
appropriate cooking dish.
7. Cook in halogen oven on lower rack at 220°C / 440°F for 15 to 25
minutes or until cooked, time will vary on what type and size of the abread
you make. (When using a regular oven pre-heat first and follow method
above until cooked.)

11

Handy Hint
Melt some butter with thyme and pour over the top to preserve the Pâté.

Chicken Liver Pâté with Apricots

Ingredients
250g / ½ lb chicken livers
½ medium onion (finely chopped)
50g / 2oz butter
8 dried apricots (finely chopped)
Salt & pepper
1 tbsp mango chutney
¼ tbsp oil
3 tbsp double cream
½ tsp thyme
Serves 5

Method

1. Chop the chicken livers in half, and place onto a round oven tray. Drizzle with oil, season and mix with the chopped onions.
2. Cook on high rack at 250°C / 500°F for eight minutes on each side. Add half the butter and cook for a further one minute or until all cooked.
3. Allow to cool and place in fridge to chill.
4. Put the cooked chicken livers, mango chutney, the rest of butter, double cream in a food processor with a mincing blade. Season again if necessary. Mix until desired consistency then stir in apricots.
5. Place the mixture in small ramekin dishes and flatten. Melt a little butter and thyme together then pour over the pâté to seal it. This way it will keep in a fridge for three days. (When using a regular hob, place in a hot frying pan and cook as method above).

13

Instead of curry powder you can use 1/2 tsp ground cumin, 1/4 tsp ground cinnamon, 1/4 ground coriander, 1/4 tsp ground cayenne pepper.

Curry Wedges

Ingredients
2 medium potatoes cut into wedges
1 tbsp curry powder
A pinch garlic salt
1 tbsp sweet chilli sauce
Salt and pepper
3 tbsp olive oil
Serves 2
Serve with sour cream and mayonnaise dip.

Method

1. Place the potato wedges, curry powder, garlic salt, sweet chilli sauce, salt and pepper to taste and olive oil in a large bowl. Mix well.
2. Place the marinated wedges on a round oven tray.
3. Place on low rack on full heat at 250°C / 500°F for 25 minutes, stirring occasionally or until cooked.
4. Serve with sour cream and mayonnaise dip, mixed together with some fresh chives. (When using a regular oven pre-heat on high and cook following the method above.)

Handy Hint
Other fillings: salami, tuna ,sweetcorn, cooked chicken, spinach, cooked mince beef, sausage, bacon, mozzarella, ham and pineapple.

French Bread Pizza

Ingredients

1 French stick
3 tbsp tomato purée
Pinch of mixed dried herbs
6 tbsp tomato sauce
1 onion finely (chopped)
3 slices/rashers bacon
10 medium mushrooms (sliced)
2 cups / 8 oz / 220g grated cheddar
1 tsp olive oil
Serves 4
Serve with rocket / arugula salad
and balsamic dressing.

Method

1. Place the chopped onion and bacon on a tray and drizzle with oil. Cook for 8 mins on the high rack at 240°C / 460°F.
2. While this is cooking, mix the tomato sauce, mixed dried herbs and tomato purée in a bowl.
3. Spread this over the sliced french bread. Top the bread with the cooked onions and bacon. Sprinkle with grated cheese and mushrooms and season.
4. Grill on a high rack 240°C / 460°F. for 10 minutes or until golden brown. Serve with rocket / arugula salad and balsamic dressing. (When using a regular grill, place on high heat, until cooked.)

17

Handy Hint
Larger peeled tiger or king prawns can be used instead.

Garlic and Sweet Chilli Prawns

Ingredients

180g / 7oz prawns
1 tbsp butter, melted
¼ tbsp honey
2 tbsp sweet chilli sauce
2 cloves garlic finely chopped
Salt & pepper
Pinch paprika
1/4 tbsp finely chopped ginger
Juice of half a lime
Serves 2
Serve with crusty bread and salad.

Method

1. Place uncooked peeled prawns into a large bowl.
2. Add butter, honey, sweet chilli sauce, garlic, salt, pepper, paprika, ginger and ¼ of the juice of the lime and mix. Leave to marinate for ten minutes.
3. Place on round oven tray or preferred dish on the top rack of halogen oven on high heat 250°C / 500°F for ten minute each side or until cooked.
4. Finish with the rest of the lime juice and serve with crusty bread and salad. (If using a regular hob, place in a hot frying pan and cook following method above).

19

Handy Hint
**Great as a main course with
stir fry vegetables.**

Garlic with Scallops and Shrimp

Ingredients

250g / 10 oz prawns / shrimps
8 scallops
4 tiger prawns
1 tbsp butter (melted)
1 tbsp vegetable oil
2 cloves garlic (finely chopped)
Salt and pepper
1 tbsp ginger (finely chopped)
Juice from lime
Serves 4

Method

1. Place the uncooked seafood into a large bowl and add butter, vegetable oil, garlic, salt, pepper, ginger and ¼ of the juice of one lime and mix. Leave to marinate for ten minutes.
2. Place on round oven tray or preferred dish, then on high rack on high heat 240°C / 500°F for ten minutes each side, or until cooked.
3. Finish with a squeeze of lime and salad.
(To cook on a regular oven, place in a hot pan until cooked.)

21

Handy Hint
Variations in place of Vermouth:
Balsamic vinegar
White wine or Brandy.

Garlic Mushrooms

Ingredients

250g / ½ lb medium sized mushrooms (washed)
3 cloves garlic (finely chopped)
75g / 3 oz butter (melted slightly)
1 tbsp parsley (chopped)
Salt and pepper
1 tbsp white Vermouth (optional)
Serves 2
Serve with salad and french crusty bread.

Method

1. Mix all ingredients together in a bowl, then place on a round tray or preferred oven dish on the high rack in the halogen oven. Cook on high heat 235°C / 450°F for 12 minutes stirring half way through the cooking time.
2. Serve with salad and french crusty bread.
(If using a regular oven pre-heat or use a hot frying pan, cook following method above).

Handy Hint
To make a dip mix 1 tbsp of mayonnaise
1 tbsp of mustard and 1 tbsp of cooked
leftover sauce.

Honey and Mustard Chicken Wings

Ingredients
12 chicken wings
2 tbsp Dijon mustard
1 tbsp English mustard
2 tbsp honey
Salt & pepper
1 tbsp lemon juice
1 tbsp brown sugar
Serves 2 / 3
Serve with salad.

Method

1. Mix the honey, mustards, lemon juice, salt and pepper together and pour over wings. Sprinkle with brown sugar and marinate for ten minutes.
2. Place on round tray on a high rack and cook on 250°C / 500°F for 20 minutes or until cooked turning half way through the cooking time.
3. Serve with salad.
(If using a regular oven pre-heat and cook following method above).

25

Handy Hint
Serve with salsa and sour cream.

Quesadillas

Ingredients

2 flour tortilla wraps
3 tbsp chilli cheese (grated)
½ red onion (sliced)
1 tbsp tomatoes (diced)
½ red pepper (sliced)
50g Cooked beef or chicken (diced)
Pinch salt
Pinch pepper
Serves 2
Serve with salad.

Method

1. Place a flour tortilla wrap on a round oven tray.
2. Add red onion, diced tomatoes, sliced red peppers, cooked chicken and grated chilli cheese.
3. Place in halogen oven on the high rack and cook on high heat 250°C / 500°F for 6 minutes then, add another tortilla wrap to form a sandwich and cook for a further 1 minute.
4. Slice into quarters like pizza and serve with salad.
(When using a regular oven, place in the grill on high heat until cooked.)

Handy Hint
Try alternative fillings:
tuna sweetcorn, chives,
ham, spicy sausage,
gruyere, cream cheese with
herbs and garlic.

Stuffed Potato Skins

Ingredients
2 medium baking potatoes
2 tbsp cream cheese
2 rashers bacon (sliced into strips)
2 tbsp grated gruyere cheese
Salt & Pepper
Serves 2

Method

1. Cook the baking potatoes in on low rack, on high heat for 60 minutes or until cooked turning regularly.
2. Once cooked, take out and place the bacon on a round tray on high heat 250°C / 500°F on the high rack until brown and crisp.
3. While this is cooking, cut the potatoes in two halves, scoop out the centres into a bowl. Add the cream cheese and cooked bacon to the potato, mix thoroughly season to taste. Scoop back into the potato shells, and place on the round tray. Cover in grated gruyere.
4. Place in the halogen oven on high rack on high heat, 250°C / 500°F until golden brown. (If using a regular oven pre-heat and cook following method above).

Handy Hint
Sprinkle with paprika.

Cauliflower Cheese

Ingredients

1 cauliflower (parboiled in florets)
4 tbsp crème fraîche
1 packet cream cheese (225g)
Mixed dried herbs
5 tbsp cheddar cheese (grated)
Serves 4

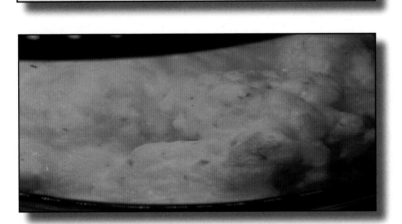

Method

1. Place cauliflower florets into a round oven dish.
2. Mix the crème fraîche with the cream cheese, mixed dried herbs and 3 tbsp of the grated cheese. Pour over the cauliflower then cover with the rest of the grated cheese.
3. Cook for 10 minutes on low rack on a high heat 250°C / 500°F until golden brown.
(When using a regular oven make sure you pre-heat the oven and follow method above).

Handy Hint
Use pork fillet instead of chicken
You can also serve with pitta and salad.

Chicken Jerk

Ingredients
1 tbsp jerk seasoning
½ tsp garlic powder
Salt & pepper
1 tbsp mango chutney
1 tbsp sunflower oil
1 tbsp mayonnaise
6 chicken thighs (boned & skinned)
Serves 3 / 4
Serve with rice, kidney beans and salad.

Method

1. Place the jerk seasoning, garlic powder, salt and pepper, mango chutney, sunflower oil and mayonnaise in large bowl. Mix thoroughly.
2. Add the chicken thighs and allow to marinate for at least ten minutes in a fridge. (Overnight is even better).
3. Cook in a round oven tray on high rack at 200°C / 400°F for 7 minutes each side or until cooked turning half way though the cooking time.
Serve with rice, kidney beans and salad.
(When using a regular oven pre-heat and follow method above).

33

Handy Hint
Add some bacon with
chicken or favourite mushrooms.

Chicken Pie

Ingredients
300g / 11 oz chicken (cubed)
1 tbsp cornflour
150ml / ¼ pt milk
150ml / ¼ pt double cream
1 chicken stock cube
1 tbsp fresh parsley
25g / 1 oz butter
Salt and pepper
4 mushrooms (sliced)
1 medium onion (chopped)
2 tsp olive oil
(Pastry)
8 oz plain flour
4 oz butter / lard or half and half
1 tbsp of water
Egg to glaze
Serves 4

Method
1. To make the pastry, place the plain flour, cold butter and lard with a drop of water into a food processor. Mix using the mincing blade, until the pastry forms a ball. Wrap the pastry in cling film and leave to rest in a fridge for thirty minutes.
2. To make the filling, put the cubed chicken pieces, onion, mushroom, olive oil, butter and seasoning in a casserole pie dish.
3. Place on lower rack on high heat 250°C / 500°F for 12 minutes, stirring twice during cooking.
4. Add the milk, saving back a little to mix with cornflour, double cream, stock cube and parsley to the chicken. Thoroughly mix cornflour with the milk, and add to filling while stirring continuously.
5. Cook for a further ten minutes on full heat 250°C / 500°F.
6. Roll out the pastry to the size of the dish, then place on top of the filling and glaze with egg. Cook for 12 minutes until golden brown, on high heat 250°C / 500°F.

Handy Hint
Great with taco and sour cream.

Chilli Con Carne

Ingredients

1lb / 500g minced beef
¼ tbsp chilli powder
1 tin kidney beans (drained)
¼ tbsp cayenne powder
1 tin chopped tomatoes
2 tbsp tomato puree
4 tbsp tomato ketchup
½ pint / ¼ litre beef stock
1 tbsp plain flour
3 medium fresh tomato (quartered)
8 mushrooms (washed and sliced)
1 onion, finely (chopped)
2 cloves garlic (finely chopped)
Serves 4
Serve with rice.

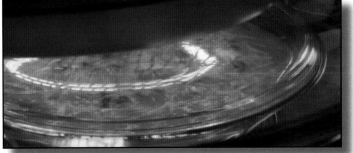

Method

1. Put the beef, onion and garlic in a large oven dish that fits into the halogen oven. Cook on the lower rack for 30 minutes at 240°C/ 440°F, until brown, stirring every 10 minutes.
2. Add chilli powder, kidney beans, cayenne powder, tinned tomatoes, tomato puree, tomato ketchup, fresh tomatoes, the mushrooms and mix in the flour. Then add the beef stock and stir in well.
3. Cover chilli with a lid, cook for 1½ hours at 180°C / 350°F, or until cooked, stirring every twenty minutes. Serve with rice.
(When using a regular oven preheat and follow method above).

Handy Hint
Serve with new potatoes, carrots, asparagus.

Cod with a Herb Crust

Ingredients

2 medium cod fillets
4 tbsp breadcrumbs
2 tbsp fresh parmesan (grated)
1 tbsp fresh parsley (chopped)
2 tbsp olive oil
1 tbsp fresh lemon juice
Serves 2

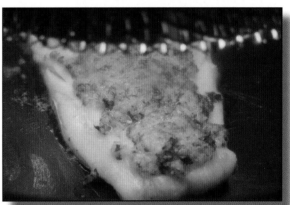

Method

1. Mix the breadcrumbs, cheese and parsley together in a bowl. Add oil and lemon juice to make a paste.
2. Place the cod fillets on a round lightly greased or oiled oven dish, Place the paste on top of the fish, covering evenly.
3. Place in halogen oven on high rack for 12 minutes at 240°C / 440°F, or until cooked.
(When using a regular oven, place in the grill on high heat follow method above until cooked).

Handy Hint
Serve with new potatoes and vegetables.

Gammon Steak with Honey and Roasted Apple

Ingredients

1 gammon steak
1 apple (quartered)
1 tbsp honey
Serves 1

Method

1. Place gammon on a round baking tray with the apple.
2. Drizzle honey over the gammon and apple.
3. Place on high heat on the high rack for 5 minutes each side.
(When using a regular oven, place in the grill on high heat alternatively hot frying pan, follow method, until cooked.)

Handy Hint
Great with cranberry sauce.

L.A. Burgers

Ingredients

500g / 1lb turkey mince
½ tsp ground cinnamon
1 onion finely chopped
1 tbsp fresh coriander (finely chopped)
1 egg
1 tbsp / 25g plain flour
Salt & pepper
Serves 4

Method

1. Place turkey mince into a large bowl and add cinnamon, onion, coriander / cilantro, egg, flour, salt and pepper. Mix and form into patties.
2. Place on a plate and cover. Rest in a fridge for an hour to help them set, then cook on the high rack on high heat 250°C / 500°F for 8 minutes each side or until cooked.
3. Serve in a bun or lettuce (or with both) with pickles, tomatoes and onions.
(When using a regular oven, place in the grill on high heat alternatively cook in a hot frying pan or until cooked).

Handy Hint
In the final stages of roasting
cover lamb joint in mint jelly.

Leg of Lamb with Rosemary and Garlic

Ingredients

900g / 2lb leg of lamb
2 sprigs of rosemary
1 whole garlic bulb (top cut off)
5 potatoes
2 sweet potatoes
1 red onion
1 butternut squash
1 tbsp oil
Salt & pepper
Serves 4

Method

1. Place the lamb on the low rack, cover with rosemary. Place the garlic on its stalk next to the leg; drizzle all with oil, cook on full heat 240°C / 460°F for 10 minutes.
2. Cut the vegetables into chunky pieces (4-5cm), drizzle with oil and season.
3. Turn the lamb over, add the vegetables cook for a further 40 minutes 180°C / 350°F, or to personal preference (pink medium well done), turning regularly.
4. Turn again and cook for a further 30 minutes at 180°C / 350°F, turning regularly or cook until how you like it.
(When using a regular oven, pre-heat and follow method above).

45

Handy Hint
You can use pepperoni
instead of bacon and add
fried onions.

Macaroni Cheese

Ingredients
8oz / 200g dried macaroni pasta
500ml boiling water
1 stock cube
5 oz / 125g cheese (grated)
3 tbsp / 75g cream cheese
Salt and pepper
2 rashers bacon (thinly sliced)
1 tbsp cornflour
3 tbsp milk
Pinch sugar
Mixed herbs
Serves 4

Method

1. Put the macaroni pasta in an oven dish, place this on the low rack.
Pour boiling water over the pasta until covered.
2. Add the stock cube and sliced bacon. Cook on full heat 250°C / 500°F
for 20 minutes.
3. Quickly stir in the cream cheese and cornflour pre-mixed with a little
milk. Add half the grated cheese and season with salt and pepper. Mix in
dried herbs and a pinch of sugar.
4. Cook for a further 10 minutes, stir and add remaining cheese on top,
and cook for another 10 minutes on 180°C / 350°F until cheese is
golden brown.

Handy Hint
Serve with bean salad.

Mexican Tuna Steaks

Ingredients
 2 raw tuna steaks
2 tbsp Tequila optional
4 spring (sliced)
Juice and zest of one lime
Salt and pepper
Serves 2
Salad and rice.

Ingredients
 (tomato salsa)
3 tomatoes (chopped & deseeded)
2 spring onions (sliced)
2 tbsp olive oil
Salt and pepper
1 tbsp lime juice
1 Jalapeno pepper (sliced)
1 tbsp coriander (chopped)

Method

1. Place tuna in a bowl and add tequila, spring onions, zest, juice of lime and season. Marinate for 10 minutes.
2. Place on a round tray on high rack and full heat 250°C / 500°F, time depends on how you like your tuna, cook accordingly.
Tomato salsa:
1. Place all ingredients into a bowl and serve with the tuna, salad and rice. (When using a regular oven, place in the grill on high heat or alternatively use a hot frying pan follow method above, until cooked.)

49

Handy Hint
Use scallops and prawns
instead of monkfish.

Monkfish Kebabs with Chilli and Lime Marinade

Ingredients
4 metal or wooden pre-soaked skewers
250g / ½lb monkfish (cut into cubes)
1 red pepper (cut into 1 inch squares)
1 large onion (cut into 1 inch squares)
¼ tsp mixed herbs
1 tbsp olive oil
Juice of a whole lime
1 tbsp sweet chilli sauce
Serves 2
Serve on a bed of rice and salad.

Method

1. Place the cubed monkfish into a bowl and add sweet chilli sauce, mixed herbs, olive oil and half the lime juice.
2. Mix and leave to marinate for ten minutes, then place on skewers with the onion and the red pepper.
3. Place on a grill tray on high rack, high heat 240°C / 440°F for 6 minutes on each side or until cooked.
4. Use the rest of the juice of the lime on the monkish and serve on a bed of rice and salad. (When using a regular oven place in the grill on high heat alternatively use a hot frying pan follow method above until cooked.)

51

Handy Hint
Great in pitta or with cous cous.

Moroccan Lamb

Ingredients

1 tbsp curry powder
2 dried apricots (chopped)
250g /10 oz lamb steak (cubed)
½ red onion (sliced)
100g / 4 oz raisins
1 tbsp pinenuts
sprig coriander to garnish
2 tomatoes (deseeded & diced)
Serves 2
Serve with cous cous and coriander.

Method

1. Place the cubed lamb in a bowl with apricots, onions, curry powder, tomatoes, raisins and pinenuts. Leave to marinate for 10 minutes.
2. Put the mixture on a round baking tray on the high rack at high heat 250°C / 500°F. Cook for 6 minutes on each side or until cooked.
3. Serve with cous cous and coriander.
(When using a regular oven pre heat and follow method above or until cooked.)

Top Tip. For a more authentic flavour add 5 grams of mixed spice to the curry powder.

53

Handy Hint
Add sweet chilli to marinade
and serve with noodles.

Oriental Salmon

Ingredients
2 salmon fillets
½ tbsp sesame seed oil
1 tbsp hoisin sauce
2 tbsp soy sauce
½ tbsp ginger (peeled & finely chopped)
¼ tbsp garlic (finely chopped)
2 Pak Choi (leaves broken off)
4 spring onions (sliced)
Serves 2
Serve on a bed of rice.

Method

1. Place salmon in a bowl and add the hoisin sauce, soy sauce, ginger, spring, sesame seed oil, garlic and mix. Leave to marinate for ten minutes.
2. Place the pak choi on the lower rack in the base of the halogen oven and cover up to the rack with boiling water. On the higher rack place the marinated salmon in an oven dish and pour over remaining marinade. Cook on 250°C / 500°F (highest temp) for 12 minutes or until cooked how personal preference. Serve on a bed of rice.
 (When using a regular oven, place in the grill on high heat or alternatively use a hot frying pan follow method above until cooked.)

Handy Hint
Pasta can be pre-cooked to save time
so you only need but you need ½ pint / ¼ litre
boiling water.

Pasta Bake

Ingredients
8 oz / 200g dried pasta shells
1 tbsp olive oil
1 stock cube
1 tin chopped tomatoes in juice
3 tbsp tomato sauce / ketchup
1 medium onion (finely chopped)
8 medium mushrooms (sliced)
2 bacon rasher (sliced thinly)
1 tin condensed tomato soup
¼ tsp mixed herbs
3 oz / 75g grated cheese
Serves 4

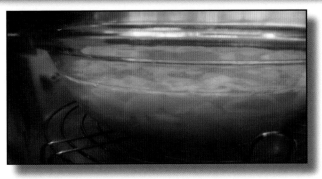

Method

1. Put onion, mushrooms, olive oil, mixed herbs and bacon in an oven dish that you are going to cook the pasta bake in and place in the halogen oven on low rack, cook on full 250°C / 500°F for 6 minutes.
2. Add pasta to the dish and cover with boiling water, stock cube and mix. Make sure the pasta is submerged and cook for twenty minutes at 250°C / 500°F, stirring twice during cooking time.
3. Add tomatoes and tomato sauce / ketchup mix. Cook for further 5 minutes at 250°C / 500°F.
4. Add the tin of soup and cover top with cheese. Cook at 180°C / 350°F for 10 minutes or until golden brown .
(When using a regular oven, make sure you pre-heat the oven and follow method above).

57

Handy Hint
Use basil and pinenuts in place
of sundried tomatoes.

Pork Chops With Parmesan and Sundried Tomato Stuffing

Ingredients
2 pork chops
8 new potatoes
Mange tout x 2 servings

Stuffing
4 tbsp bread crumbs
1 tbsp fresh parmesan (grated)
4 sundried tomatoes, (finely chopped)
Pinch of mixed herbs
Salt & pepper
2 tbsp of olive oil or (oil from the sundried tomatoes)
Serves 2

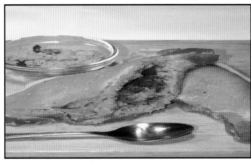

Method

1. Start cooking the new potatoes round the edge of the oven on the low rack for 5 minutes on 240°C/ 460°F.
2. Combine breadcrumbs, Parmesan, salt and pepper, mixed herbs, sundried tomatoes and oil in a bowl to form a paste.
3. Slice pork chops to make pockets. Do not cut all the way through. Fill the pockets with the stuffing mix and place chops on the top rack. Brush with oil and cook on a high temperature 240°C / 460°F for 20 minutes, turning half way through the cooking time.
4. Five minutes before the end of cooking, open the halogen oven, take out the top dish, add one inch of boiling water in the base with the mange tout. Replace the dish and carry on cooking, this way everything will be ready at the same time. (If using a regular oven pre-heat and follow method above cooking the mange tout separately).

59

Handy Hint
Great served with
humous and olives.

Pork Pittas

Ingredients

200g / 8oz pork loin
1 tbsp mango chutney
½ onion (finely chopped)
½ tbsp curry powder
¼ tsp cumin powder
1 red pepper (diced)
Pinch garlic salt
1 tbsp oil
Serves 2
Serve with red onion and green
salad within a pitta bread.

Method

1. Cut loins into 1cm thick rounds, flatten into a large circle with a mallet.
2. Mix marinade by combining onion, red pepper, mango chutney, cumin, curry powder, garlic salt and oil. Add to pork loin and marinate for ten minutes.
3. Cook on a high rack on round oven tray, at 250°C / 500°F for 6 minutes each side.
4. Serve with red onion and green salad within a pitta bread.
(When using a regular oven place in the grill on high heat alternatively cook in a hot frying pan, follow method above, until cooked.)

**Handy Hint
Add some lemon zest
to the butter.**

Posh Fish and Chips

Ingredients

1 sea bass
   (gutted, head & fins removed)
1 lemon
1 tsp dried dill
1 tsp parsley (chopped)
1 potato (cut into chips)
50g / 2oz butter
1 tbsp oil
Pinch sea salt
Serves 1
**Serve with slightly grilled,
skinned cherry tomatoes.**

Method

1. Mix butter with chopped parsley and dill.
2. Score the fish twice and fill with the butter, parsley and dill.
3. Cover potato chips in oil and season.
4. Place chips on a baking tray for 13 minutes on high rack at high heat 250°C / 500°F, turning approximately every 4 minutes.
5. Place fish on same tray and cook for 6 minutes each side or until cooked, not forgetting to turn chips.
6. Serve with slightly grilled, skinned cherry tomatoes.
(When using a regular oven, pre-heat and follow method above, until cooked.)

63

Handy Hint
Once the sausage and potato is cooked mix up six eggs and pour over. Cook to make a spanish omelette.

Potato and Sausage Breakfast

Ingredients
1 cubed potato
2 tomatoes (halved)
½ onion (sliced)
4 sausages or chorizo sausage
¼ tsp mixed herbs
1 tbsp vegetable oil
1 tsp olive oil
Salt and pepper
Serve with 2 fried eggs & toast
Serves 2

Method
1. Put the sausages on a round tray on the high rack and cook at 225°C / 450°F for 3 to 4 minutes each side, until golden brown. Remove and slice.
2. Place onions, potatoes, vegetable oil and seasoning in the tray and put back in oven on high, 225°C / 450°F for 25 minutes, stirring every 5 minutes.
3. In the last five minutes put the sliced sausages back into the mixture, and put the halved tomato brushed with olive oil and herbs on the top.
4. Serve with toast and a fried egg, which can be done in the halogen oven also (cook on a tray on high rack to your taste).
(When using a regular oven, pre-heat and follow method above.)

65

Handy Hint
Serve on a bed of rice
with a tomato and onion
salad, naan bread and
mango chutney.

Quick Tandoori Masala Chicken

Ingredients
2 tbsp tandoori masala seasoning
12 mini chicken fillets
3 tbsp natural yoghurt
¼ tbsp fresh ginger (finely chopped)
2 garlic cloves (crushed)
Salt and pepper
2 tsp sunflower oil
½ Red onion (sliced)
¼ tbsp cumin seeds
Juice half lime
Serves 4

Method

1. Place chicken fillets, tandoori masala seasoning, natural yoghurt, ginger and garlic in a large bowl. Season with salt and pepper, add oil, onion, cumin seeds and juice of half a lime.
2. Leave to marinate for ten minutes in fridge.
3. Place on round oven tray and place in halogen oven on high rack at full heat 250°C / 500°F for 10 minutes on each side or until cooked.
4. Serve on bed of rice, tomato, onion salad, naan bread and mango chutney.
(When using a regular oven, place in the grill on high heat alternatively hot frying pan. Follow method above, until cooked.)

67

Handy Hint
Can be served with mash and steamed vegetables.

Rack of Lamb with Garlic and Rosemary

Ingredients
2 sprigs of rosemary
4 cups ready made instant gravy
1 tbsp red currant jelly
1 tbsp garlic slithers
Salt & pepper
Serves 4

Method

1. Score lamb and use a knife to make small insertions into skin.
then add the rosemary and garlic slithers into the insertions.
2. Rub with salt.
3. Place on lower rack on full heat for 250°C / 500°F 30 minutes, turning every 10 minutes.
4. Continue cooking if required to personal taste and season.
5. Add red currant jelly to the hot gravy, stir and serve.
(When using a regular oven pre heat and follow method above, until cooked.)

69

Handy Hint
Great with grilled / roasted meats and rice.

Ratatouille

Ingredients

1 tin chopped tomatoes
2 tbsp tomato puree
1 red onion (sliced)
1 aubergine / eggplant (cubed)
1 courgette / zucchini (sliced)
1 red pepper (large diced)
Pinch mixed herbs
Serves 4

1 yellow pepper (large diced)
1tbsp pine nuts
1tbsp olive oil
Salt and pepper
½ tbs chopped garlic
3 tbsp tomato ketchup
½ pt / ¼ litre vegetable stock

Method

1. Add the red onion, aubergine, tomato puree, courgette, red pepper, yellow pepper, pine nuts, olive oil, salt and pepper, mixed herbs and garlic to an oven proof casserole dish and mix thoroughly.
2. Place in halogen oven on lower rack and cook on high heat 240°C / 440°F stirring every 5 minutes for 20 minutes, so the vegetables are starting to roast as this will really add to the flavour.
3. Add the tin of tomatoes and stir in the ketchup and vegetable stock to make to the consistency you require.
4. Stir every 5 minutes and cook for a further 20 minutes on temperature 200°C / 390°F.

(If using a regular oven, pre-heat and cook following method above.)

Handy Hint
Works well with rib of beef, also
a diffrent variety of mushrooms can be
used.

Roast Beef with Porcini Mushrooms and Red Wine Gravy

Ingredients
900g / 2lb beef joint
25g / 1oz dried porcini mushrooms
125ml / ¼ pt red wine
1 onion (finely chopped)
1 heaped tbsp cornflour
 (mixed with little cold water)
1 tbsp butter
¼ tbsp gravy browning
1 beef stock cube
Salt & pepper
Serves 4

Method
1. Soak the porcini mushrooms in 300ml / ½ pint of hot water with beef stock cube. Rub salt on the beef joint.
2. Place onion, red wine, porcini mushrooms in water and stock in base of halogen bowl. On the lower rack place the the beef joint and cook for 20 minutes at 240°C / 460°F and turn every 10 minutes.
3. Add butter and gravy browning, cornflour to the bottom of the halogen bowl and stir.
4. Cook for a further 30 minutes for medium rare, turning every 10 minutes at 180°C / 350°F. Continue for a further 20 minutes or longer for well done, season to taste. (When using a regular oven make sure you pre-heat the oven and follow method above).

73

Handy Hint
You can use diced fresh apple instead of cranberry.

Roast Chicken with Sage and Cranberry Stuffing

Ingredients
1 medium chicken
Salt and pepper to taste
Stuffing ingredients
5 tbsp breadcrumbs
½ onion (chopped)
2 tbsp cranberry jelly
1 egg
¼ tbsp dried sage
½ tbsp oil
Serves 4

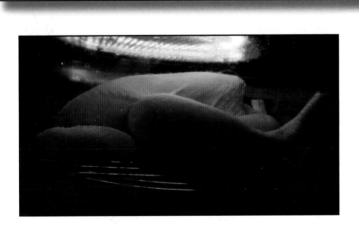

Method

1. Rub chicken skin with salt and pepper, and place on low rack in halogen oven. Cook for 45 minutes turning every 10 minutes at 220°C/440°F, then turn it down to 180°C / 360°F for the rest of the cooking time (about another 45 minutes or until cooked).
2. Mix together stuffing ingredients and place in a ramekin dish, place in oven next to chicken for the last 25 minutes of cooking.
(When using a regular oven, pre-heat and follow method above).

75

Handy Hint
For shredded crispy duck rolls, first boil the duck in water with ¼ tsp Chinese five spice and 1 tbsp soy sauce for 1 hour. Then follow the method from the start, and serve with pancake rolls, cucumber, spring / green onion and plum / hoisin sauce.

Chinese Roasted Duck

Ingredients

1 half duck
1½ tbsp Chinese five spice
2 bacon rashers
4 tbsp orange marmalade
  (or apricot jam)
2 tbsp soy sauce
2 tbsp sesame oil
Salt & pepper
Serves 2
Serve with cooked noodles
and pak choi.

Method

1. Wrap bacon around the end of the
leg and wing so they don't burn, rub duck with salt and ½ tbsp five
spice.
2. Cook in the oven for 15 minutes each side on a low rack,
210°C / 405°F.
3. Mix marmalade, 1 tbsp five spice, soy sauce, sesame oil and brush
over duck skin. Cook for a further 20 minutes, or until cooked to your
satisfaction.
4. Serve with cooked noodles and pak choi.
(When using a regular oven, pre-heat then follow method above.)

Handy Hint
Use apple or apricots instead of peaches.

Roast Pork With Peach Stuffing

Ingredients

900g / 2 lb pork chop joint

Stuffing ingredients

125 g / 5 oz bread crumbs

¼ tbsp mixed herbs

1 onion (finely chopped)

1 tin peaches in halves

Salt and pepper

Serves 4

Serve with steamed vegetables and roast potatoes.

Method

1. Place the breadcrumbs, mixed herbs, onion and ½ half a peach (finely chopped) together with some of the peach juice in a bowl and mix to form a stuffing. Make a hole in the centre of your pork joint and fill with the stuffing. Rub the top of the pork joint with salt, place on a roasting tray on the lower rack of the halogen oven.

2. Cook for 1 hour turning every 15 minutes, at 220°C / 440°F. Then cook for another 30 minutes at 180°C / 360°F and put the peaches and the rest of the juice round the pork joint. Season again with salt and pepper.

3. Check that the pork joint is cooked all the way through, if not cook at 180°C / 360°F until ready.

Serve with steamed vegetables and roast potatoes.

(When using a regular oven, pre-heat first then follow method above, until cooked).

79

Handy Hint
Serve with grilled meats.

Roasted Vegetables

Ingredients

1 carrot, (peeled & sliced)
1 red onion (peeled & cut into 8)
1 red pepper(de seeded & sliced)
1 butternut squash (de seeded & sliced)
1 courgette / zucchini (sliced)
1 sweet potato (sliced)
20 cherry tomatoes
¼ tbsp celery salt
¼ tsp garlic puree
Salt and pepper
2 tbsp olive oil
4 sprigs fresh thyme
Serves 4

Method

1. Place all ingredients into a large a bowl and mix, then place in a round roasting tray.
2. Place on lower rack on high heat 250°C / 500°F stirring about every 5 minutes for 30 minutes.
(When using a regular oven, pre-heat then follow method above, until cooked.)

81

Handy Hint
Serve with crushed peanuts.

Satay Chicken

Ingredients
Juice of ½ lime
8 mini chicken fillets
1 tbsp curry powder
2 tbsp peanut butter
1 tbsp mango chutney
1 tbsp mayonnaise
1 tbsp sweet chilli sauce
Serves 4
Serve on a bed of rice and steamed vegetables.

Method

1. Place peanut butter into a bowl, place on high rack in halogen oven for 1 minute to soften, then add curry powder, mango chutney, mayonnaise, sweet chilli and lime juice.
2. Mix in chicken fillets strips and allow to marinate for 10 minutes.
3. Place on round oven tray on high rack and cook on a high heat 250°C / 500°F for 16 minutes turning half way through the cooking time.
Serve on a bed of rice and steamed vegetables.
(When cooking in a regular oven, pre-heat oven and follow method above, until cooked.)

83

Handy Hint
You can also add scallops.

Seafood Bake

Ingredients

150g / 6 oz cooked prawns
150g cod fillet
1 tbsp cornflower
¼ ltr / ½ pt milk
50g / 2 oz butter
50ml double cream
1 chicken stock cube
Pinch of garlic salt
Pinch salt and pepper
2 tbsp fresh parsley (chopped)

Crumble mix

100g / 4oz plain flour
50g / 2oz butter
Salt and pepper
2 tbsp parsley (chopped)
2 slices of whole grain bread crumbs
75g / 3oz Gruyère cheese (grated)

Serves 4

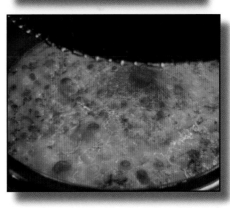

Method

1. Place cod, salt & pepper, milk, garlic salt, stock cube, fresh parsley and butter in an oven dish on low rack on on high heat 250°C / 500°F for 25 minutes.

2. With a wooden spoon break the cod into flakes. Mix the cornflower in a cup with a little water until it becomes liquid, adding some of the flavoured milk from the oven dish. Stir the contents of the cup back into the oven dish.

3. Add prawns and double cream and cook for a further 10 minutes on high heat 250°C / 500°F. While this is cooking, use a food processor with the mincing blade to mix flour, butter, salt, pepper, fresh parsley, whole grain bread and gruyère cheese. Mix until it resembles breadcrumbs.

4. Stir filling and top with crumble mix. Cook until golden brown on high heat 250°C / 500°F. (When cooking in a regular oven, pre-heat oven and follow method above.)

85

Handy Hint
To make more spicy
add your favourite
chilli sauce.

Spicy Meat Loaf

Ingredients

550g / 1¼ lb minced / ground beef
6 tbsp bread crumbs
½ tsp cayenne pepper
1 egg
2 tbsp sour cream / yogurt
2 tbsp tomato ketchup
Mixed dried herbs
1 onion, chopped
Salt & pepper
½ tbsp Worcestershire sauce
Serves 4
Serve with peas, onion rings and mashed sweet potatoes.

Method

1. Place the beef, bread crumbs, egg, sour cream, tomato ketchup, mixed dried herbs, onion, Worcestershire sauce, cayenne pepper and salt and pepper into a large mixing bowl and mix well.
2. Place in a large loaf tin and pat down to form a loaf.
3. Cook on the low rack for twenty minutes on 240° / 440°F, then cover with foil and carry on cooking on 190°C / 360°F for 30 minutes or until cooked.
Serve with peas, onion rings and mashed sweet potatoes.
(When using a regular oven, pre-heat and follow method above).

87

Handy Hint
Serve with rice or
tortilla wraps

Stir Fry Chicken with Ginger and Soy Sauce

Ingredients

½ tbsp ginger (finely chopped)
2 cloves garlic (finely chopped)
3 spring onions (sliced)
4 chicken thighs(skinned & de boned)
2 tbsp sweet chilli sauce
½ tbsp soy sauce
8 mushrooms (sliced in quarters)
1 red pepper (sliced)
1 carrot (peeled and sliced diagonally)
Salt pepper
½ tbsp sesame seed oil
Serves 4
Serve on a bed of rice with steamed pak choi

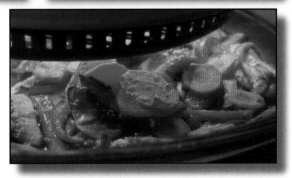

Method

1. Place the ginger, garlic, spring onions, chicken thighs, chilli sauce, soy sauce, mushrooms, peppers, carrots, sesame seed oil, salt and pepper in a large bowl mix and season. Allow to marinate for 10 minutes.

2. Place all the mixture on a round oven tray on the high rack in halogen oven. Set to high heat 250°C / 500°F and cook for about 20 minutes stirring every 5 minutes.

Serve on a bed of rice with steamed pak choi, this can be cooked at the same time as the chicken by placing underneath the chicken in a little boiling water.

(Stir fry can be cooked in a wok following the method above).

Handy Hint
Use whole grain mustard in the butter instead of thyme.

Steak with Thyme Butter

Ingredients

1 sirloin steak
1 tomato cut in half
3 new potatoes
40g / 1 oz butter
Pinch mixed herbs
1 tbsp thyme leaves
1 tbsp of oil
Serves 1
Serve with a green salad

Method

1. Cut the potatoes into wedges, season and coat with ½ the oil, put on a round tray on the low rack and cook with high heat 250°C / 500°F for 15 minutes.
2. Move the tray of wedges up to the high rack and add the steak and carry on cooking for 5 minutes on each side or to your taste. Season steak.
3. Brush tomatoes with remaining oil, season and sprinkle mixed herbs on top. Add to the tray and cook for a further 2 minutes. When cooked, serve with a green salad and top with blended butter and thyme leaves.

Handy Hint
Can use thinly sliced chicken or prawns
instead of cod.

Sweet And Sour Cod

Ingredients

2 skinless cod fillets
2 tbsp tomato sauce
1 tbsp sugar
1 tbsp mango chutney
1 tbsp vinegar
225g tinned pineapple in juice
½ green pepper
½ onion cubed
1 tbsp oil
1 tbsp cornflower
        Serves 2

Method

1. Place cod & oil on round oven tray and season, put in halogen oven on high rack 240°C / 440°F for 6 minutes turning once.
2. In a bowl add tomato sauce, sugar, mango chutney, vinegar, pineapple, green pepper, onion and cornflower (pre-mixed with a little cold water).
3. Mix well then pour over the cod and cook for a further 10 minutes stirring twice.
4. Serve on a bed of rice.
(When using a regular oven place in the grill on high heat alternatively cook in hot frying pan, follow method above, until cooked.)

Handy Hint
You can use fresh peaches cut in half, instead of pineapple, and garnish with fresh basil leaves.

Baked Pineapple

Ingredients
1 pineapple, quartered
4 tbsp rum
2 tbsp dark brown sugar
Serves 4
Serve with Créme Fraîche
or ice cream.

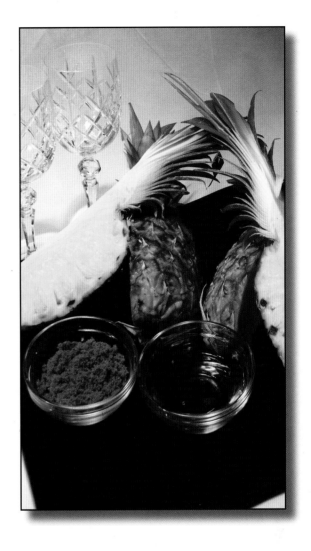

Method

1. Score pineapple quarters to form cubes.
2. Mix rum and brown sugar together.
3. Pour over pineapple.
4. Place the pineapple on the high rack at 180°C / 350°F
for 10 minutes

(If using a regular oven pre-heat and cook following method above).

95

Handy Hint
Can use blue berries or
black berries, or milk
chocolate.

Cheats Crème Brûlée

Ingredients

1 can of custard
24 raspberries
2 tbsp brown sugar
8 squares white chocolate
Serves 4

Method

1. In 4 ramekins place the raspberries and two chocolate squares.
2. Pour custard into ramekins.
3. Sprinkle the tops with brown sugar.
4. Place on top rack in the halogen oven on a high heat 250°C / 500°F until sugar has caramelised and serve while still hot.
As an alternative cooking method, use a blow torch to brown the top of the crème brûlée.

Handy Hint
Use brandy instead of rum.
Instead of ice cream used thick cream.

Hot Bananas with Rum and Raisin

Ingredients

4 bananas
2 tbsp rum
2 tbsp raisins
12 milk chocolate squares
Chocolate sauce
Vanilla ice cream
4 tin foil squares
Serves 4
Serve with ice cream covered
with chocolate sauce.

Method

1. Place the bananas over a square of tin foil, then slice an opening along the bananas and fill with chocolate and raisins and sprinkle with rum.
2. Close the tin foil and cook on high rack at 250°C / 500°F for 8 minutes or until hot. Place on plate and serve with ice cream covered with chocolate sauce.

Handy Hint
You can use
white chocolate
instead of milk
chocolate.

Chocolate Indulgence

Ingredients

100g / 4oz self raising flour
100g / 4oz butter
100g / 4oz caster sugar
3 eggs
100g / 4oz coco powder
100g / 4oz chocolate chips
4 tbsp chocolate sauce
8 milk chocolate squares
Serves 4
Serve on a plate with ice cream or thick cream.

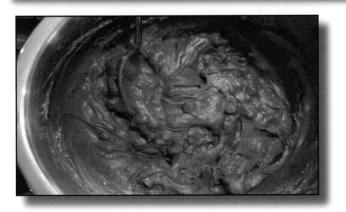

Method

1. Mix the flour, butter, caster sugar, eggs, coco powder and chocolate chips in a large bowl with a wooden spoon or in a food mixer.
2. Butter 4 ramekins and place chocolate sauce and chocolate squares in the bottom, then cover with the cake mix.
3. Place the lower rack in the base of the halogen oven and cover just below the rack with boiling water. Then place the ramekins on the rack and cook on 150°C / 300°F for 40 minutes or until cooked.
4. Serve on a plate with ice cream or thick cream.
(When using a regular oven pre heat and follow method above, but put a tray with some water in oven to keep the cake moist.)

Handy Hint
Add raisins or sultanas
instead of pecans.

Maple and Pecan Sticky Pudding

Ingredients

6 tbsp maple syrup
12 pecan nuts
125g / 5 oz butter
100g / 4 oz self raising flour
100g / 4 oz brown sugar
2 eggs
4 ramekin dishes greased
Serves 4

Method

1. Mix the sugar and butter together then add the egg and flour, stirring and beating constantly until well mixed.
2. Add half the pecan nuts and 2 tbsp of the maple syrup .
3. In the base of the ramekin dishes place the rest of the pecan nuts, maple syrup, then place the cake mix on top.
4. Place a cup of boiling water in the base of the Halogen oven. Cover with tin foil, place on the lower rack and cook at 170°C / 340°F for 45 minutes or until cooked. Turn upside down and remove from ramekin to serve. (When using a regular oven, pre-heat and follow method above, until cooked.)

Handy Hints
Why not try using
dried apricots and cranberries
as an alternative.

Oat Flapjack

Ingredients
225g / 9 oz oats
75g / 3 oz butter
50g / 2 oz brown sugar
50g / 2 oz golden or maple syrup
pinch salt
50g / 2 oz dried fruit
Serves 6

Method

1. Mix all ingredients together. Place a cup of boiling water in the base of the Halogen oven.
2. Place ingredients onto a greased baking tray on the low rack. Cook at 180°C / 360°F for 25 minutes or until cooked. Allow to cool a little and cut into sections.

Handy Hint
You can use other fruit
(apricots, peaches, pineapple or apple)
instead of pears..

Pear Upside Down Cake

Ingredients

Sponge mix
4 oz / 100g self raising flour
4 oz / 100g butter
2 eggs
4 oz / 100g caster sugar
Base
3 tbsp golden / maple syrup
1 oz / 25g butter
5 glacé cherries
Tinned pear halves, drained
Serves 4-6

Method

1. Mix sponge ingredients in a food mixer until creamed together well, alternatively mix with a wooden spoon in a large bowl.
2. Put the golden syrup, butter, glacé cherries and tinned pears in the base of a 8" or 20cm cake tin or similar. Place the cake mix on top.
3. Place a cup of boiling water in the base of the Halogen oven. Place the tin in the halogen oven on the lower rack, with the higher rack on top with the heat diffuser / steam rack to diffuse the heat. Or if you have not got one of these, place the higher rack on top and cover with a piece of tin foil, punched with lots of holes, just to slow down the cooking process on the top of the cake. Cook at 180°C / 360°F for 45-55 minutes or until cooked.
4. Turn out when cooked, upside down, on a plate.

107

Why we love Halogen Oven Cooking

In times gone by many years ago, before electricity in the home, kitchens always had a big oven heated by fire, but you also had the big open fires with the roasting spit-hand crank (rotisserie) in front for such things as roasting lamb, suckling pig and roasting chickens, as well as other birds.

The reason for this was radiant heat energy. Its intense heat sealed the meat on the outside making it succulent and juicy on the inside. This helped to render down the fat, so the meat was not sitting in it. This makes it better for you than in an oven where it is required for extra fat to be added to the baking tray, to stop the meat from drying out and often sitting in the fat.

The Halogen Oven is a modern day method of achieving similar results to spit roast and open fire roasting effortlessly.
This is why we love Halogen cooking!

Conversion For Recipes From A Regular To Digital Halogen Oven

If your halogen oven has pre-set temperatures please follow the temperature chart below. With the fan speed I find it is best to use it on full speed

150°C = 150°C
160°C = 150°C
175°C = 180°C
180°C = 180°C
200°C = 205°C
210°C = 205°C
225°C = 235°C
240°C = 235°C
250°C = 260°C
Always check your food is cooked before you take it out .

Crisp & Bake

For cooking in the "Crisp & Bake" always cook on the low rack and add a little extra time if necessary. Always follow the manufacturers instructions for use and cleaning.

Rotisserie Halogen Oven

If you are using a "Rotisserie Halogen Oven" and the maximum heat setting is lower than the recipes states, adjust the cooking time for a bit longer until properly cooked.

Top tips for your halogen oven

1) When steaming vegetables always use boiling water in the base of your oven to save time on heating up. Place the boiling water in first before turning the cooker on. I tend to put vegetables on the low rack and put the high rack on top with the round oven tray and fill with boiling water which will generate the steam when the halogen heat hit the water, the fan above then moves the steam round the cooker. I steam at 140°c 280 f.

2) When grilling such things as bacon you can put tin foil in the base, or before you start cooking add a cup full of water to the base of the halogen oven bowl, then any dripping fat floats on the top of the water and doesn't stick to the bowl. Making it easier to clean.

3) As a rough rule when cooking meat joints on the low rack, I tend to start on a high heat to seal the meat. This keeps the juices in. Then lower to the temperature required. When cooking things that you want well done, I use the extender ring to make the cooking process more gentle. This will cook the meat more evenly. I also tend to turn joints during cooking.

4) When cooking casseroles, always use an oven dish that fits in the halogen bowl so air can circulate round. In this dish, fry off the meat first with the vegetables. Then I add the liquid and cover with foil wrap. I have also used oven proof glass lids to keep the liquid in and stop it from drying out. Then I turn down the temperature as I would in a regular oven.

All temperatures given are a rough guide, always check the food has been thoroughly cooked before consumption, especially poultry and pork.

INDEX A-Z

S
Satay Chicken 83
Seafood Bake 85
Spicy Meat Loaf 87
Spicy Pork Pitta 61
Steak with Thyme Butter 91
Stir Fry Chicken With Ginger and Soy Sauce 89
Stuffed Potato Skins 29
Sweet and Sour Cod 93

Halogen Cooking Made Simple....

Paul Brodel & Dee Hunwicks